THE LITTLE BOOK OF
SOUPS

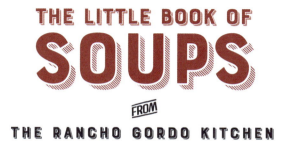

FROM

THE RANCHO GORDO KITCHEN

THE LITTLE BOOK OF
SOUPS

FROM

THE RANCHO GORDO KITCHEN

Photography: Howard Hsu and Steve Sando
Project editor: Julia Newberry
Book design: Alexandra Zeigler
Production design: Diana Heom
Production management: Chris Hemeseth

With thanks to Anita Epler Crotty for copyediting and Ken Della Penta for indexing. Special thank you to Nancy Aguilar, Monica Casillas-Gutierrez, Diana Arriaga, Alejandra Castro, Alondra Chavez, and Kelani Steward for help in the test kitchen.

ISBN 979-8-218-69320-6
Printed in China on FSC Certified Paper

MIX
Paper | Supporting
responsible forestry
FSC® C102842

10 9 8 7 6 5 4 3 2
First edition

Rancho Gordo Press
1350 Main Street
Napa, CA 94559
www.ranchogordo.com

CONTENTS

INTRODUCTION

"Only the pure of heart can make good soup" — Beethoven

It's a strange fellow who doesn't welcome a bowl of hot, delicious soup, lovingly made in a happy kitchen. It's an obvious choice for winter, but some of the world's great soups come from countries that rarely dip into sweater weather.

In this little book, we honor soup in all its glory, with a special accent on soup made with beans, lentils, and garbanzos. We've gone through our archives, begged recipes from friends, and tested new soups in our Rancho Gordo test kitchen and the result is *The Little Book of Soups*.

"Whenever something went wrong when I was young — if I had a pimple or if my hair broke — my mom would say, 'Sister mine, I'm going to make you some soup.' And I really thought the soup would make my pimple go away or my hair stronger." — Maya Angelou

For making soup, we often will start with sautéed onions and garlic. Like so many dishes, this is a great way to start things. Once soft, add some vegetables and then add stock of some kind. Bean broth is a kind of stock and you can use it pure, or cut it with water, chicken stock, or vegetable stock.

If you simmer things too long, they can get murky and unpleasant but it often takes hours to get to that point. On the other hand, in general, it's nice to simmer a mix of things for soup for at least 15 minutes.

Beans are a natural in soup, as the base and as an ingredient. Beans and mushrooms; beans and grains like wild rice or farro; beans and chicken or beef; beans and whatever is hanging around in your refrigerator's vegetable bin...there's no limit.

There is no shame in using ingredients just past their prime. That's one of the miracles of soup. Not only is it delicious, but it's practical and you just become a better cook every pot you make.

— STEVE SANDO, RANCHO GORDO

COOKING WITH HEIRLOOM BEANS

We're often torn on the best way to organize our cookbooks: by season, by dish, or by ingredient? Since legumes are always the stars of our show, we've chosen to organize this book by legume type: white and light beans; medium and dark beans; and other legumes.

Rather than starting with a specific recipe and choosing a bean to match, we suggest cooking a pot of beans first and letting them guide your meal. If you've cooked a pot of white beans and are in the mood for a soup, head to that chapter for some ideas. You can always tweak the ingredients based on the season or your dietary preferences.

WHITE AND LIGHT BEANS

ALUBIA BLANCA
This small, versatile Spanish-style white bean has a creamy texture and thin skin but still manages to hold its shape.

AYOCOTE BLANCO
A super-rich midsize white bean, Ayocote Blanco holds its shape through long cooking but manages to stay creamy. A versatile runner bean.

CASSOULET (TARBAIS)
West Coast–grown from classic French Tarbais seed stock, it's the most famous bean for a traditional cassoulet but versatile enough to become an everyday favorite.

FLAGEOLET
A super-mild European-style classic heirloom bean, known for pairing with lamb but excellent as a pot bean and with roasted tomatoes.

LARGE WHITE LIMA
Lima beans have a creamy texture and savory flavor and they taste more like fresh vegetables than other beans. New-crop Large White Lima beans are quick-cooking and delicious and worthy of your attention, especially if you grew up eating those nasty frozen Lima beans.

MARCELLA (CANNELLINI)
Grown from heirloom Italian seed, this thin-skinned cannellini is named after Italian cooking hero Marcella Hazan, who encouraged our growing it. A delicate tribute to a mighty force of nature.

ROYAL CORONA
An enormous, thick-skinned runner bean with a surprisingly creamy interior. One of our all-time best sellers, it's a versatile giant that works in all kinds of cuisines. A true pantry staple.

MEDIUM-BODIED BEANS

BUCKEYE
Small, dense yet velvety bean that holds its shape and provides a rich bean broth. Easily one of the staff's favorite beans.

CRANBERRY
Versatile and velvety, this thin-skinned Borlotti bean produces a rich, indulgent bean broth, making it perfect for classic Italian dishes as well as simple pot beans.

EYE OF THE GOAT
Our famous bean with velvety texture and deep bean broth. A favorite classic pot bean that needs little adornment.

GOOD MOTHER STALLARD
Deep rich flavor, velvety texture, and an addictive bean broth make Good Mother Stallard almost everyone's favorite bean.

KING CITY PINK
A medium-size pink heirloom bean from King City, California, with a rich history and a dreamy bean broth. It has a thin skin and a dense yet creamy interior.

MAYOCOBA
Creamy and versatile, Mayocoba has a pale yellow hue and super soft texture. This mild-flavored bean soaks up all the flavors of the cooking pot.

PINTO
The classic bean. Soft, creamy, and versatile, our Pintos cook quickly and create converts to new crop, heirloom beans.

SANTA MARIA PINQUITO
The small, dense orbs produce a beefy bean broth. An essential ingredient in California cuisine, it's the heart of a tri-tip barbecue and yet perfectly at home in meatless meals.

YELLOW EYE
Rich, creamy, and mild, this best-seller is delicious without fuss. Essential for New England baked beans but versatile enough for almost any cuisine.

DARK AND HEARTY BEANS

AYOCOTE MORADO
This thick-skinned purple bean, produced in Mexico, is pretty and very large. It's starchy but goes from dense to creamy with continued cooking.

AYOCOTE NEGRO
Nearly identical to Ayocote Morado in size, texture, and flavor, Ayocote Negro beans are jet black.

CHRISTMAS LIMA
A rich chestnut texture and an almost nutty flavor make this the most unusual Lima bean. A true revelation for those who believe they don't like Lima beans.

DOMINGO ROJO
A classic red bean, essential to dishes like New Orleans red beans and rice, and equally important to many Caribbean cuisines. Domingo Rojo holds its shape when cooked, and the thick bean broth coats every rice grain or noodle with a luxurious sauce.

MIDNIGHT BLACK
A versatile, essential black turtle bean. It holds its shape through lots of cooking yet retains its famous creamy interior. The bean broth can be used as a base for all kinds of soups.

MORO
Beautiful markings and a dense, rich flavor make this super-rare bean a favorite. Almost a marriage between a black bean and a Pinto but unique in its own right.

REBOSERO
An heirloom passed down for generations in rural Hidalgo, Mexico, this compact bean produces a rich, flavorful broth.

RIO ZAPE
The heirloom bean that inspired the birth of Rancho Gordo. Suggestions of chocolate and coffee make this Pinto family rarity one of our favorite and most requested beans.

SCARLET RUNNER
Big, beefy runner bean with gorgeous markings. Cooks from starchy to creamy and is a constant chef's favorite.

VAQUERO
A classic chili bean that holds its shape through long, slow cooking and exudes a generous, dark, rich broth.

OTHER LEGUMES

BLACK EYED PEAS
All good Southerners and their friends know the secret to a prosperous New Year (and beyond) is to eat old-fashioned Black Eyed Peas on New Year's Day. Cooking new-crop peas from Rancho Gordo ensures that your years will be tastier, as well.

GARBANZO BEANS
A slightly nutty-flavored classic bean, essential for Middle Eastern, Mexican, and European cooking. Garbanzos aren't indigenous to the Americas, but we love them so much and the imported crops tend to be so old and dusty that we make this one of our California crops.

GREEN SPLIT PEAS
A quick-cooking and nostalgic legume, a bowl of split pea soup is a happy bowl indeed. It's time to bring green split peas back into the spotlight! They cook up quickly and produce a delicious thick, comforting soup with or without pork. It's a classic with ham bits but it's just as delicious made with a few aromatic vegetables and water.

LENTILS
At Rancho Gordo, we ignored lentils for years, but we will ignore them no longer! They were one of humanity's earliest cultivated crops and have been a source of sustenance for thousands of years. History aside, what we love about them is that they are quick cooking, they taste delicious, and they only need a few aromatic vegetables and a splash of good olive oil to make a great meal. From tiny, inky Black Caviar Lentils to hearty French Green Lentils to Masoor Dal (Split Red Lentils), they all offer endless soup inspiration.

COOKING A POT OF BEANS
IN THE RANCHO GORDO MANNER

There's no right way to cook beans, and there's only one actual rule: Simmer the beans in a pot until they're soft.

Soaking can speed up the process. Adding broth, seasonings, or vegetables will make the beans more flavorful. It's really that simple. There are different methods and small changes you might make, but basically, this is it.

Heirloom and heritage bean varieties don't need a lot of fussing so long as they're used within 2 years of harvest. We usually start with a classic mirepoix — a mix of onion, celery, and carrot, all diced fine — sautéed in some kind of fat, often olive oil. A crushed garlic clove doesn't hurt.

Add the beans and their soaking water to a large pot. You probably were taught to change the water and rinse the beans, but current nutritional wisdom holds that vitamins and flavor leech out of the beans into the soaking water, which you end up throwing down the drain. There's some conflicting scientific evidence as to whether or not changing the water cuts down on the digestive gas that eating beans can produce. It's your choice: If you want to get rid of the soaking water, do it; if it seems unnecessary, don't bother.

If you've soaked the beans, they will have expanded, so make sure they are still covered by a couple inches of water in the pot. Add the sautéed vegetables to the beans and give everything a good stir. Increase the heat to medium-high and bring the liquid to a rolling boil. Keep the beans boiling for 10 to 15 minutes. This is the moment that really matters: You have to give the beans a good, hard boil to let them know you're the boss, then reduce them to a gentle simmer before covering. Open and close the lid, or keep it ajar, to help control heat and allow some evaporation. The bean broth will taste its best if it has had a chance to breathe and reduce a little.

The aroma will fill the room when the beans are almost ready. You'll no longer smell the vegetables you've cooked, but the beans themselves. At this point, go ahead and salt them. Go easy on the salt at first, and taste the beans after a bit more cooking; it takes a while for them to absorb the salt. If you want to add tomatoes, or acids like lime juice or vinegar, wait until the beans are cooked completely.

If the bean water starts getting low, always add hot water. Many cooks believe that cold water added to simmering beans will harden them. We're not convinced, but it will make the cooking take longer, because you'll need to bring the beans back to a simmer. We don't recommend using hot tap water, though; It's better to heat cool tap water in a kettle or saucepan first.

After patiently waiting, simmering, and tasting for tenderness, you're done! Once you've mastered this method, go ahead and try a few different techniques, if you like. Your bean-loving friends will swear by this or that method. Try them, if you want, keeping in mind there are few absolutes. It's hard work to mess up a pot of beans, as long as you're paying attention.

COOKING BEANS IN A SLOW COOKER

Every day at Rancho Gordo, our retail staff cooks a batch of our heirloom beans in the Crock Pot for customer samples. This is how they do it.

1 pound Rancho Gordo beans

2 garlic cloves, finely chopped

½ of a small onion (preferably white), finely chopped

1 tablespoon extra-virgin olive oil

1 tablespoon dried Mexican oregano, preferably Rancho Gordo Oregano Indio

1 tablespoon kosher salt

Check beans for small debris and rinse in cool water. Depending on how much time you have, you can soak the beans or cook them right away. Soaking the beans will reduce the cooking time. If you choose to soak, cover the beans with cool water and soak for 4 to 6 hours.

Place the beans in the slow cooker and cover with about 2 inches of water. Add the garlic, onion, and olive oil. Add the oregano, crushing it with your hand to release the flavor before adding it to the pot.

Put the lid on the slow cooker and cook the beans on high for 3 to 4 hours for soaked beans, or 4 to 5 hours for unsoaked beans. Check the beans occasionally for doneness to avoid overcooking. Add salt when beans are just starting to soften.

COOKING BEANS IN A PRESSURE COOKER

It's best to consult the manufacturer's instructions for your pressure cooker's preferred bean-cooking method. If your manual's lost in the junk drawer, this is the basic idea, although you may need to experiment with timing and ratios to discover what works best.

Place cleaned beans in the pressure cooker and add enough water to cover by about 2 inches. Cook under pressure for 20 to 40 minutes, depending on size and age of beans; release pressure naturally. Simmer with the lid off for another 20 minutes.

WHITE *AND* LIGHT BEANS

CREAMY LIMA BEAN, TOMATO, AND FETA SOUP

This soup was born of leftovers in a refrigerator: Beans, tomatoes, Valbreso French sheep-milk feta, and an immersion blender.

Our beans were well-seasoned and the salt content of feta can vary wildly. If you don't have Valbreso, try traditional feta, but it will be different — and likely saltier. We like whole peeled tomatoes but crushed would work, although Steve seems to think they have a slightly metallic flavor. However you end up making it, hot tomatoey-bean soup is in your future.

¼ of a white onion, chopped

1 tablespoon extra-virgin olive oil, plus more for garnish

1 garlic clove, minced

Salt and freshly ground black pepper

1½ cups cooked Rancho Gordo Large White Lima beans or other white beans

2 to 3 canned whole peeled tomatoes, roughly chopped

½ cup crumbled French feta cheese, preferably Valbreso brand

2 to 3 cups bean broth and/or vegetable broth

½ teaspoon Rancho Gordo Oregano Indio, plus more for garnish

In a small soup pot, sauté the onion in the olive oil over medium heat for about 5 minutes. Add the garlic and a small pinch of salt. Cook, stirring occasionally, until just soft, about 10 minutes. Add the beans, tomatoes, and cheese; cook for an additional 5 minutes.

Stir in 2 cups of broth; cook for 5 minutes. Puree the soup with an immersion blender in the pan until smooth (or transfer half the mixture to a food processor or blender, and process in batches before returning to the pan). Season to taste with salt and pepper. Add more liquid if needed, then stir in the oregano.

Ladle into individual bowls. Drizzle with olive oil and garnish with additional oregano.

Serves 2 to 4

ST. VALENTINE'S BEAN AND BEETROOT SOUP

The texture of this soup is velvety and the flavor is rich. There are no tomatoes — the color and flavor come from cooked beets and vegetables. Any Rancho Gordo white bean you have on hand is suitable.

---

1 large beet, peeled and quartered

2 celery stalks, roughly chopped

2 small carrots, peeled and scrubbed, roughly chopped

½ of an onion

3 garlic cloves, peeled and smashed

6 tablespoons extra-virgin olive oil, plus more for garnish

2 teaspoons Herbes de Provence

1½ cups cooked Rancho Gordo white beans, such as Marcella, Alubia Blanca, or Royal Corona

1 cup chicken or vegetable stock

Salt and freshly ground black pepper

Chopped parsley, for garnish

In a medium stock pot over high heat, add the beets, celery, and carrot. Cover with water and bring to a boil for 5 minutes. Lower the temperature to medium-low, partially cover, and continue to simmer until all of the vegetables are soft, about 20 minutes.

Strain the vegetables, reserving the broth and the vegetables separately.

In the same pan over medium heat, sauté the onion and garlic in olive oil until soft, about 7 minutes, stirring occasionally. Add the Herbes de Provence, followed by the reserved vegetables and the beans. Stir to combine, then add 4 cups of the reserved vegetable broth and 1 cup of chicken or vegetable stock for a total of 5 cups of liquid. (Add more water if needed to bring the total to 5 cups.)

Puree the soup with an immersion blender in the pan until smooth (or transfer half the mixture to a food processor or blender, and process in batches before returning to the pan). Season to taste with salt and pepper, and simmer over medium heat for 20 minutes.

Serve in individual bowls, topped with chopped parsley and drizzled with olive oil.

Serves 4 to 6

CHARRED CABBAGE AND
CARAMELIZED SHALLOT SOUP
WITH ROYAL CORONA BEANS

CHARRED CABBAGE AND CARAMELIZED SHALLOT SOUP WITH ROYAL CORONA BEANS

We've been following and admiring Chef Pierce Abernathy's Instagram feed, and we adapted one of his soups using white beans instead of potatoes. It's a winner. With so few ingredients, each one has the chance to shine.

1 small head of cabbage, preferably savoy, outer leaves removed

4 tablespoons extra-virgin olive oil (divided use), plus more for drizzling

Salt and black pepper

8 to 10 shallots, peeled and sliced

4 cups vegetable broth

5 cups cooked Rancho Gordo Royal Corona or Cassoulet beans, with about 2 cups of their broth

Zest from 1 large lemon (divided use)

Minced parsley, for garnish

Cut the cabbage in half, then cut each half into 3 or 4 wedges, leaving the core intact.

Warm a skillet over medium-high heat. Add 2 tablespoons oil and swirl to coat the surface of the skillet. Add the cabbage wedges; season with a pinch of salt and pepper. Let the cabbage cook undisturbed for about 5 minutes, or until the bottom side is well blackened. Flip the cabbage and season the second side with a pinch of salt and pepper. Cook undisturbed for about 5 minutes, or until the bottom side is well blackened. Remove the cabbage wedges and set aside. Once cool enough to handle, roughly chop and reserve.

Wipe the skillet clean, then warm the remaining 2 tablespoons oil over medium-low heat. Add the shallots and a sprinkle of salt; cook, stirring occasionally, until completely soft and caramelized, 10 to 15 minutes. Set aside.

Add the vegetable broth plus 3 cups beans and 2 cups bean broth to a large soup pot. Puree with an immersion blender until smooth (or transfer to a blender or food processor and process in batches before returning to the pot). Place the pot over medium heat and bring to a simmer. Stir in the chopped cabbage, caramelized shallots, and remaining beans. Add more broth if desired. Cook for 10 to 15 minutes to combine the flavors. Stir in most of the lemon zest, leaving some for garnish. Taste and adjust seasonings, as needed. Garnish with parsley, remaining lemon zest, and a drizzle of olive oil; serve warm.

Serves 4

FISH AND SHRIMP STEW WITH ALUBIA BLANCA

The inspiration for this came from *Acquacotta*, a book on Tuscan coastal cooking by Emiko Davies (Hardie Grant, 2017). The original recipe calls for clams and no fish, but sometimes you have fresh prawns and white fish on hand. When it comes to seafood, you can be flexible.

The stew can be made ahead a day or two, up to the point of adding the fish and prawns. You can reheat the pot the next day and, once simmering, add the seafood.

¼ cup extra-virgin olive oil

2 yellow onions, thinly sliced into half-moons

2 celery stalks, thinly sliced

Salt

2 garlic cloves, peeled and smashed

1 teaspoon Rancho Gordo New Mexican Red Chile Powder

28-ounce can whole peeled tomatoes

2 cups water

1½ cups cooked Rancho Gordo Alubia Blanca or other white beans

1 to 2 pounds halibut or another sturdy white fish, cut into cubes

1 pound shrimp, peeled and deveined

1 bunch flat-leaf parsley, roughly chopped

4 to 6 thick slices stale (or toasted) rustic bread

Lemon wedges, for serving

In a large pot over low heat, warm the oil. Add the onions, celery, and a pinch of salt; cook, stirring occasionally, until the vegetables are soft, about 20 minutes. Don't allow the onions to brown. Add the garlic and chile powder; sauté for a minute.

Empty the can of tomatoes into a bowl and break up the tomatoes into small pieces with your hands. Add to the simmering pot along with the water. Stir and gently simmer for 30 to 40 minutes.

Add the beans and stir to combine. Taste and adjust seasoning, as desired. Bring the pot back to a simmer and add the fish and shrimp. Cook until seafood is done, 2 to 5 minutes. Remove from heat and stir in the parsley. Place a piece of bread in the bottom of each bowl, and carefully ladle the stew over the bread. Serve with lemon wedges.

Serves 4 to 6

WHITE BEAN AND TOMATO SOUP FOR A STORMY NIGHT

There's nothing like rain and thunder to inspire one to stay home and eat soup. This recipe finds its inspiration from a cold, Northern California evening with nothing prepared to eat but a fridge full of good cooked Ayocote Blanco beans and, on the counter, a local multi-grain sourdough bread that had started to go south.

Adding langostino tails, or another type of seafood, is not necessary but an indulgent option if you happen to have seafood on hand.

¼ of a white or yellow onion, chopped

¼ cup extra-virgin olive oil, plus more for garnish

3 garlic cloves, minced

2 small carrots, cubed

1 celery stalk, cubed

1 teaspoon Herbes de Provence

Salt

3 canned whole peeled tomatoes, roughly chopped

2 roasted red peppers, chopped

1 cup bean broth

2 cups chicken or vegetable broth

1 parmesan cheese rind (optional)

About 12 ounces langostino tails (or cleaned and deveined shrimp), defrosted if frozen (optional)

1 to 2 cups cooked Rancho Gordo Ayocote Blanco or other white beans

Homemade Croutons (page 98) (optional)

In a small soup pot over medium heat, sauté the onion in the olive oil for about 5 minutes. Add the garlic, carrots, celery, Herbes de Provence, and a small pinch of salt. Cook, stirring occasionally, until just soft, about 15 minutes. Add the tomatoes and roasted red peppers; cook for an additional 5 minutes.

Add the broths and stir to combine; cook for 5 minutes. Puree the mixture with an immersion blender in the pan until smooth (or transfer half to a food processor or blender, and process in batches before returning to the pan). Taste and adjust salt, if needed. Add the parmesan rind, if using, and continue to cook over medium heat, partially covered, for about 20 minutes. The soup should maintain a gentle simmer.

Add the langostino tails, if using, and gently simmer until cooked through. Add the beans and cook until warmed through. Ladle into individual bowls. Drizzle with olive oil and top with croutons, if using.

Serves 2 to 4

WHITE BEAN CHOWDER WITH SWEET POTATOES AND SAGE

Cassoulet beans have a neutral flavor and a soft texture, making them naturals for chowder. Serve this soup with a thick slice of crusty bread and a smear of butter for a winter meal. A version of this recipe first appeared in *Heirloom Beans* by Steve Sando and Vanessa Barrington (Chronicle Books, 2008).

2 to 3 tablespoons olive oil

1 large yellow onion, diced

2 celery stalks, diced

3 garlic cloves, chopped

1 pound uncooked Rancho Gordo Cassoulet, Yellow Eye, or Cranberry beans, picked over and rinsed

2 small Garnet sweet potatoes, peeled and diced (about 2 cups)

½ pound chicken sausage, cubed or crumbled

2 tablespoons chopped fresh sage

Salt and freshly ground black pepper

Chopped flat-leaf parsley, for garnish

In a large soup pot, warm the olive oil over medium heat. Add the onion, celery, and garlic; sauté until soft and fragrant, about 10 minutes. Add beans and enough water to cover beans by 2 inches. Increase heat to high and bring to a rolling boil over high heat; cook for 10 to 15 minutes. Simmer, partially covered, until about half done: the beans should still be fairly firm with some give.

Add the sweet potatoes, sausage, sage, salt, and pepper. Reduce heat to a gentle simmer and cook, stirring occasionally, until beans are tender but not falling apart. Serve immediately, garnished with chopped parsley.

Serves 6 to 8

HEARTY TUSCAN RIBOLLITA WITH MARCELLA BEANS AND KALE

It's amazing how many great bean recipes come from Italy. You can find different versions of this soup all over Tuscany, but black kale, or cavalo nero, is a classic ingredient. This kind of kale is often labeled in the U.S. as dinosaur or lacinato kale. A version of this recipe first appeared in *Heirloom Beans* by Steve Sando and Vanessa Barrington (Chronicle Books, 2008).

½ cup extra-virgin olive oil (divided use)

1 medium yellow onion, chopped

1 celery stalk, chopped

3 garlic cloves, finely chopped

1 medium carrot, peeled and chopped

4 cups shredded savoy cabbage

1 bunch dinosaur kale, tough stems removed and leaves coarsely chopped

6 cups chicken broth

Salt and freshly ground black pepper

2 cups drained, cooked Rancho Gordo Marcella beans, or other white beans

6 slices day-old hearty bread, each about ½-inch thick, cut from a large loaf

½ cup freshly grated Parmesan cheese

In a soup pot over medium heat, warm ¼ cup of the olive oil. Add the onion, celery, garlic, and carrot; sauté until soft and fragrant, but not brown, about 10 minutes. Add the cabbage and kale; sauté until well coated and beginning to wilt. Add the broth and season with salt and pepper. Bring to a simmer, cover, and cook until the cabbage and kale are soft, about 1½ hours. The soup is even better made up to this point 1 to 3 days ahead and refrigerated, then rewarmed for serving.

Preheat the oven to 400°F.

With the soup at a slow simmer, add the beans. Cook for 15 minutes to blend the flavors. Taste and adjust seasoning, as desired. Line the bottom of a 3- or 4-quart Dutch oven or ovenproof baking dish with 2 of the bread slices. Top with half of the soup, and layer 2 more bread slices on top of the soup. Add the remaining soup and the remaining bread slices, pushing down to submerge them in the liquid. Drizzle the top evenly with the remaining ¼ cup olive oil. Top with parmesan cheese. Bake until the top is brown and bubbly, 20 to 25 minutes. Ladle into warmed bowls and serve.

Serves 4 to 6

PANCETTA, CORN, AND BEAN SOUP

Between the farmers markets, a vegetable garden, and sloppy refrigerator provisioning, one can end up with too many vegetables. If you find yourself with excess corn, try a soup like this with pancetta, Rancho Gordo Cassoulet beans, and corn fresh off the cob.

If you prefer creamier soups, you can obviously blend this with an immersion blender. For the liquid, we like a mix of bean broth and water. The pancetta and aromatics make such a delicious base that you don't need much else as long as the corn is fresh and the beans are good.

1 tablespoon olive oil

3 ounces pancetta, cubed

3 garlic cloves, minced

½ of a yellow onion, chopped fine

2 to 3 ears of corn, kernels removed

1 tablespoon Rancho Gordo Oregano Indio

2 cups cooked Rancho Gordo Cassoulet or Marcella beans, plus 1 cup of their broth

2 to 3 cups water

Salt and freshly ground black pepper

2 to 3 tablespoons heavy cream (optional)

Minced flat-leaf parsley or cilantro, for garnish

In a soup pot, warm the olive oil over medium-low heat. Add the pancetta; sauté until tender and chewy, about 10 minutes, stirring occasionally to prevent burning.

Add the garlic and onion; sauté until soft, about 5 minutes. Add the corn, oregano, beans an broth, and 2 cups of water, stirring to combine. Increase heat to medium and continue cooking, stirring occasionally, until corn is tender and flavors have blended, about 20 minutes. Add more water if desired.

Season with salt and pepper. Right before serving, you can add some heavy cream, if you like, and cook another 2 or 3 minutes to warm through. Serve in bowls, garnished with fresh herbs.

Serves 4

SENATE BEAN SOUP

This soup was made famous in Washington, D.C. The official recipe calls for Navy beans, but we think Rancho Gordo Alubia Blanca or Yellow Eye beans make it a superior dish.

1 pound Rancho Gordo Alubia Blanca, Yellow Eye, or Flageolet beans, picked over and rinsed

1 pound smoked ham hocks

2 tablespoons butter

½ of a medium onion, chopped

1 celery stalk, chopped

1 garlic clove, minced

Salt and freshly ground black pepper

Chopped parsley, for garnish (optional)

In a large pot over high heat, add the beans and enough water to cover by about 2 inches. Bring to a rolling boil for 10 to 15 minutes, then reduce the heat to low. Add the ham hocks and gently simmer, stirring occasionally, until beans are soft and soup is thick and creamy, about 1½ hours. Add more water as needed to keep the beans and ham submerged.

Remove the ham hocks and set aside. When cool enough to handle, dice meat and return to the soup.

Meanwhile, in a skillet over low heat, melt the butter. Add the onion, celery, and garlic; sauté until the vegetables are tender, about 10 minutes. Stir the vegetable mixture into the soup, reduce the heat to low, and cook for another 45 minutes, adding up to 2 more cups of water if the soup is too thick. Season to taste with salt and pepper. Garnish with parsley, if desired.

Serves 4 to 6

WHITE BEAN AND CAULIFLOWER SOUP WITH ROSEMARY CROUTONS

If you have cooked white beans and stale bread, might we suggest a pureed white bean soup? It's easy to adjust the ingredients depending on what you have on hand: Start by sautéing aromatic vegetables and herbs in olive oil or butter, then add a hearty vegetable like cauliflower, along with broth and cooked beans. Simmer until tender, blend to your preferred consistency, and add your favorite garnish.

---

4 tablespoons extra-virgin olive oil (divided use), plus more for drizzling

2 leeks, white and light-green parts only, well rinsed and chopped

2 garlic cloves, chopped

1 teaspoon minced fresh thyme

3 teaspoons minced fresh rosemary (divided use)

1 medium head of cauliflower, trimmed and roughly chopped

4 cups vegetable or chicken broth

3 cups cooked Rancho Gordo white beans, such as Alubia Blanca or Marcella, plus 1 cup of their broth

Salt and freshly ground black pepper

3 or 4 thick slices of rustic bread, cubed or torn into bite-size pieces

---

Preheat the oven to 400°F.

In a soup pot over medium heat, warm 2 tablespoons of the oil. Add the leeks and sauté until softened, about 8 minutes. Add the garlic, thyme, and 1 teaspoon rosemary; sauté for another minute. Add the cauliflower, vegetable or chicken broth, beans and bean broth, salt, and pepper. Bring to a boil. Reduce the heat and simmer, partially covered, until cauliflower is tender, about 20 minutes.

Meanwhile, in a bowl, toss the bread cubes with the remaining 2 tablespoons of oil, 2 teaspoons of rosemary, and a pinch of salt. Spread the bread on a rimmed baking sheet and bake until golden, about 10 minutes.

Puree the soup with an immersion blender in the pan until smooth (or transfer half to a food processor or blender, and process in batches before returning to the pan). Taste and adjust the seasonings, and add more liquid if it's too thick. Rewarm the soup if needed.

Serve drizzled with olive oil and topped with rosemary croutons.

Serves 4

WHITE BEAN SOUP WITH CORN AND POBLANO STRIPS

Say you have a couple of cups of cooked white beans in your refrigerator because you've made a big pot of beans earlier in the week. You've also roasted a batch of poblano peppers and have one left. You've got corn in the freezer, and some garlic and onion. That's a soup in the making, friends!

2 tablespoons olive oil

3 garlic cloves, minced

½ of a yellow onion, finely chopped

3 ears of corn, kernels removed (or about 1½ cups frozen corn)

1 poblano chile, roasted, peeled, and seeded (page 99), then sliced into strips

1 tablespoon Mexican oregano, such as Rancho Gordo Oregano Indio

2 cups cooked Rancho Gordo white beans, such as Alubia Blanca or Ayocote Blanco

3 cups liquid (we like half water and half bean broth)

Salt and freshly ground black pepper

2 to 3 tablespoons heavy cream (optional)

Minced flat-leaf parsley or cilantro, for garnish

Lime wedges, for serving

In a soup pot, warm the olive oil over medium-low heat. Add the garlic and onion; sauté until soft, about 5 minutes. Add the corn, poblano strips, oregano, beans, and liquid, stirring to combine.

Increase heat to medium and continue cooking, stirring occasionally, until corn is tender and flavors have blended, about 20 minutes.

Season to taste with salt and pepper. Right before serving, you can add some heavy cream, if you like. (If you do, let the soup cook another 2 or 3 minutes to warm through.) Serve in bowls, garnished with fresh herbs and lime wedges.

Serves 4

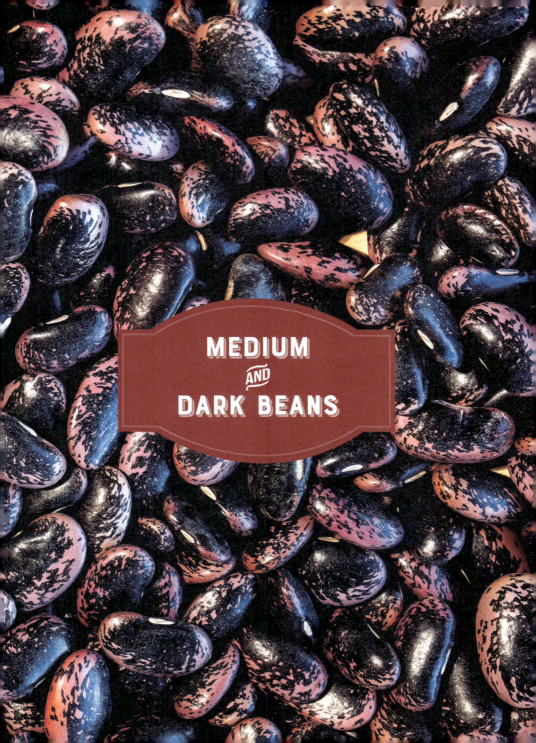

MEDIUM AND DARK BEANS

NEW ORLEANS RED BEAN SOUP WITH SAUSAGE AND COLLARD GREENS

Red Beans and Rice is an iconic New Orleans dish. This soup captures many of the same flavors, but features the addition of Black Eyed Peas and collard greens. Serve with freshly baked cornbread, if you can.

2 tablespoons olive oil

12 ounces andouille or other firm, spicy sausage, thinly sliced

1 large onion, diced

2 celery stalks, diced

1 to 2 carrots, diced

1 small red or green bell pepper, diced

2 garlic cloves, minced

2 teaspoons Cajun Seasoning (see page 98), or to taste

4 cups chicken or vegetable broth

2 cups cooked Rancho Gordo Domingo Rojo beans

1 cup whole canned tomatoes with their juice (about 4 tomatoes)

1 bunch collard greens, stemmed and chopped

1 tablespoon vinegar

2 cups cooked Rancho Gordo Black Eyed Peas

Salt

Cornbread or rolls, for serving (optional)

In a large pot over medium heat, warm the olive oil. Add the sausage and cook until browned, about 5 minutes. Add the onion, celery, carrots, and bell pepper; sauté until softened, about 3 minutes. Add the garlic and Cajun Seasoning; sauté for another minute.

Add the broth, beans, tomatoes, collard greens, and vinegar; bring to a boil. Reduce heat to low; simmer, partially covered, until the collards are soft, about 30 minutes.

Stir in the Black Eyed Peas and cook for another 5 minutes to warm through. Taste and adjust seasoning and salt.

Serve with freshly baked cornbread or crusty rolls, if desired.

Serves 4

KING TRUMPET MUSHROOM AND CHRISTMAS LIMA BEAN SOUP

Christmas Limas have a wonderful chestnut-y texture and an almost beefy flavor and broth. We think they are the perfect match for all types of mushrooms, but King Trumpet mushrooms really knocked us out. This large variety of oyster mushroom (*Pleurotus eryngii*) — sometimes known as King Brown or French Horn — are somewhat mild but they take on all the surrounding flavors. They were suggested by Connie and Staffan, our friends at Wine Forest.

The seared mushrooms are almost like little steaks. You could simmer them with the soup but we prefer adding them at the last minute to really appreciate their texture.

You are likely to have extra Leek Relish and that's a good thing. It's great on a Swedish cracker, smothering a layer of goat cheese. Or most any bowl of beans would welcome a savory plop.

Extra-virgin olive oil

6 to 7 King Trumpet mushrooms, sliced in long slim sections lengthwise, about ⅛ inch thick

1½ cups cooked Rancho Gordo Christmas Lima beans, plus 1 cup of their broth

1 cup chicken or vegetable broth

½ cup Leek Relish (page 99)

Salt and freshly ground black pepper

About 1 teaspoon freshly grated lemon zest

In a large skillet over high heat, add enough olive oil to lightly cover the surface. Cook each mushroom slice until brown on both sides, then remove to a cutting board. (It may take several batches — don't crowd the pan.) When cool, cut into large bite-size pieces and set aside.

In a medium soup pot over medium-low heat, combine the beans and bean broth, chicken or vegetable broth, and leek relish; simmer gently until warmed through, about 10 minutes.

Just before serving, add the mushroom pieces. Season to taste with salt and pepper.

After ladling into soup bowls, top with lemon zest and a drizzle of olive oil.

Serves 2

SOMEWHAT TARASCAN BEAN SOUP

A regional specialty in the town of Pátzcuaro, Mexico, Tarascan soup is most likely named for the local indigenous people, now correctly referred to as Purépecha. It's generally a combination of tomatoes, chicken stock, and pureed beans, with crispy ancho chile strips as a garnish.

This version is more tomato-heavy than most, and we used our Oregano Indio and New Mexican chile powder, which are not traditional.

2 plum tomatoes, sliced lengthwise	1 ancho chile, stemmed, seeded, and deveined (soaked in warm water for 15 minutes, if brittle)	TOPPINGS:
½ of a medium onion		3 tablespoons olive oil
1 garlic clove, peeled		1 ancho chile, stemmed, seeded, and sliced into thin strips
1½ cups cooked Rancho Gordo Pinto or Cranberry beans, drained, plus 1 cup of their broth	1 teaspoon Rancho Gordo Oregano Indio or Mexican Oregano	2 corn tortillas, cut into strips
	1 teaspoon Rancho Gordo New Mexican Chile Powder	Cotija cheese
1 cup chicken broth	2 tablespoons olive oil	Fresh cilantro
	Salt	Mexican crema or sour cream thinned with water

Heat a nonstick skillet or comal over medium-high heat. Place the tomatoes, onion, and garlic in the pan and cook, turning occasionally with tongs, until charred on all sides, 10 to 15 minutes. Remove each item to the from the pan as it's done, and transfer to a blender or food processor. Add the beans, bean broth, and chicken broth; process until ingredients are combined. Add the chile, oregano, and chile powder; puree until smooth.

In a stockpot over medium-high heat, warm the oil; add the bean mixture. Bring to a gentle boil, then reduce to a simmer; cook until the soup reaches a creamy consistency. Add salt to taste.

Heat the oil in a skillet over medium heat. Fry the ancho strips until crisp, about 2 minutes, being careful not to burn them. Remove to a paper-towel–lined tray. In the same cil, add the tortilla strips and fry until crisp, about 2 minutes; drain alongside the ancho strips.

Serve in bowls, topped with ancho strips, tortilla strips, cheese, cilantro, and crema.

Serves 2 to 3

MEXICAN SHRIMP AND CRANBERRY BEAN SOUP

This soup is inspired by Patricia Quintana's book on soup, *Sopas* (Oceano, 2012). It's the perfect way to use up that last cup or so of beans. In this case, we used our classic Cranberry bean but any Cranberry-type bean, or even Pinto beans, would work.

---

2 tablespoons olive oil

1 small onion, chopped fine

3 garlic cloves, smashed

1 teaspoon ground cumin

1 teaspoon Mexican Oregano

1 serrano chile, minced (seeded for a milder soup)

Salt

2 cups cooked Rancho Gordo Cranberry beans, plus 1 cup of their broth

14-ounce can chopped tomatoes

3 cups chicken broth

1 pound peeled shrimp

1 tablespoon butter

In a soup pot over medium heat, warm the olive oil. Sauté the onion and garlic until soft, then add the cumin, oregano, chile, and a good pinch of salt. Cook, stirring frequently, until fragrant.

Add beans and their broth, tomatoes, and chicken broth; simmer for about 20 minutes. Puree the soup with an immersion blender in the pan until smooth (or transfer half to a food processor or blender, and process in batches before returning to the pan). Taste and adjust seasoning.

When you're ready to serve, add the shrimp and cook through, about 3 to 5 minutes. Stir in the butter and serve.

Serves 2 to 4

BORLOTTI MINESTRONE WITH ARUGULA PESTO

Cranberry beans have been bred around the world and go by many names; in Italy, the Borlotti is a beloved variety. You can also use Cannellini beans, like Rancho Gordo Marcella beans, in this soup. A version of this recipe first appeared in *Heirloom Beans* by Steve Sando and Vanessa Barrington (Chronicle Books, 2008).

3 tablespoons extra-virgin olive oil

1 small yellow onion, sliced

3 garlic cloves, finely chopped

1 medium fennel bulb, trimmed and thinly sliced

Salt

½ medium head green cabbage

5 cups chicken broth

½ pound green beans, trimmed and halved

2 cups cooked Rancho Gordo Borlotti or Cranberry beans, in their broth

Freshly ground pepper

FOR THE PESTO:

3 garlic cloves

Salt

¼ pound baby arugula leaves

About ½ cup flat-leaf parsley leaves

⅓ cup extra-virgin olive oil

½ cup freshly grated Parmesan cheese

2 to 3 tablespoons fresh lemon juice

Freshly ground pepper

In a soup pot over medium heat, warm the olive oil. Add the onion, garlic, fennel, and a pinch of salt; sauté until the vegetables are soft and fragrant, about 10 minutes. Add the cabbage, stir to coat with the oil, and cook until wilted, about 5 minutes. Add the chicken broth and another pinch of salt. Bring to a boil and simmer, uncovered, for 15 minutes. Add the green beans and the Borlotti beans; simmer for 15 minutes. Season to taste with salt and pepper.

Meanwhile, make the pesto: Pound the garlic and a pinch of salt in a mortar and pestle; transfer to a food processor. (You may also use the food processor for the first step, but pounding the raw garlic makes it mellow and sweet, and creates a texture that integrates well into the pesto.) Add the arugula, parsley, and a pinch of salt. Process until well chopped. With the motor running, slowly drizzle in the olive oil, stopping once to scrape down the sides of the bowl. Stir in the Parmesan and lemon juice, and season with salt and pepper.

Ladle the soup into warmed bowls and top with a dollop of pesto. Store any leftover pesto, topped with a little more olive oil, in the refrigerator for up to 1 week.

Serves 4 to 6

GALLINA PINTA

GALLINA PINTA

This brothy hominy-and-bean stew is popular in the state of Sonora, in Northern Mexico. It is traditionally topped with chiltepín chiles, a small, spicy chile that's grown all over Sonora, but harder to find in the U.S. (You can sometimes find their domesticated twin, pequín chile, more easily.) If you can't find them and want to add some heat, you could garnish with minced serrano or habanero chile, or your favorite chile paste.

This recipe makes plenty to share, so invite some friends over!

1 gallon (16 cups) water

1½ pounds oxtail

1½ pounds chamorro (beef cross-cut hind shanks)

1 pound uncooked Rancho Gordo Pinto beans

1 medium white onion, peeled and halved (divided use)

2 small Anaheim chiles (divided use)

1 garlic head, cut across the top to expose the cloves, plus 2 garlic cloves, peeled (divided use)

2 bay leaves

1 bunch cilantro, tied with kitchen twine

2 plum tomatoes

Salt and freshly ground black pepper

7 to 8 cups cooked Rancho Gordo White Corn Posole/ Prepared Hominy (about 1 pound dry), see page 98

1 teaspoon Rancho Gordo Oregano Indio or Mexican Oregano

Chopped cilantro, onion, radish, and/or minced serrano or habanero chile, or dried chiltepín or pequín chiles, for garnish

Lime wedges, for serving

In a very large pot over high heat, bring the water to a boil. Add the beef and continue to boil, removing the foam that forms on the surface. Add the beans along with half of the onion, a whole Anaheim chile, the garlic head, bay leaves, and cilantro. Cover and cook over medium heat until the beans are just tender, 1 to 2 hours. Remove and discard the onion half, chile, garlic head, bay leaves, and cilantro.

While the beans simmer, stem and roughly chop the remaining chile and the tomatoes. In a blender, combine the chile, tomatoes, remaining onion half, garlic cloves, 1 teaspoon each salt and pepper, and 1 cup of the simmering liquid from the beef. Blend until smooth.

To the stew, add the cooked posole, oregano, and blended tomato mixture. Cover and cook for 20 to 30 more minutes to blend the flavors. Taste and adjust seasoning. Serve with desired garnishes and lime wedges.

Serves 6 to 8

CLASSIC PASTA E FAGIOLI

We are calling this a classic version of Pasta e Fagioli but there's a good chance your Italian grandmother wouldn't agree. She would add a little more of this and a little less of that. This version, adapted from our friend Dario Barbone's recipe, has become a favorite.

As you prepare beans, make sure you use plenty of liquid, as this will be the basis for your sauce. If you have less than 4 cups of bean broth, make up the difference with chicken or vegetable broth. You can substitute white beans for the Cranberry beans.

2 tablespoons extra-virgin olive oil, plus more for serving

4 ounces pancetta, cubed or roughly chopped (optional)

1 medium onion, finely chopped

1 celery stalk, finely chopped

1 carrot, minced or sliced

1 garlic clove, minced

1 tablespoon tomato paste

½ teaspoon red pepper flakes (optional)

3 cups cooked Rancho Gordo Cranberry or Borlotti beans, plus 4 cups of their broth

1 rosemary sprig

Salt and freshly ground black pepper

8 ounces good-quality pasta (we like shells or tubes)

Chopped flat-leaf parsley, for garnish (optional)

Grated pecorino or Parmesan cheese, for serving

In a medium saucepan, warm the olive oil over medium heat. If using pancetta: fry the pancetta until fragrant and chewy. Once cooked, remove with a slotted spoon and to a paper-towel–lined plate. If needed, add more olive oil to the pan so there is enough fat to fry the vegetables. Add the onion, celery, carrot, and garlic; sauté until the vegetables are soft and the onion is turning golden. Add the tomato paste and pepper flakes (if using); cook for a few minutes until the paste heats through and the tomato flavor intensifies.

Add the bean broth and rosemary; taste and adjust the salt and pepper. Gently simmer until the liquid starts to reduce, about 15 minutes.

Meanwhile, in a large stockpot, cook the pasta in salted water according to package directions. Drain well. Add the pasta, beans, and reserved pancetta (if using) to the vegetable mixture; stir to combine, and gently cook for a few minutes to marry the flavors.

Remove the rosemary sprig. Serve immediately with a splash of peppery extra-virgin olive oil and a sprinkle of parsley, if desired. Pass around a bowl of grated pecorino or Parmesan cheese for guests to help themselves.

Serves 4 to 6

KING CITY PINK BEAN AND SPANISH CHORIZO STEW

Here is a super simple, flexible soup for a quick weeknight meal. Any heirloom bean would work well. Note that we used hard, cured Spanish chorizo, which is different from the fresh Mexican-style chorizo that needs to be cooked first.

2 to 3 tablespoons extra-virgin olive oil

¼ cup minced white onion

1 cup diced cured Spanish chorizo (or to taste)

2 garlic cloves, minced

3 cups chicken or vegetable stock

1 cup tomato purée

2 cups cooked, drained Rancho Gordo King City Pink beans, or other mild heirloom beans

Salt and freshly ground black pepper

3 tablespoons vegetable oil, for frying

2 to 3 corn tortillas, cut into strips

Minced cilantro or parsley, for garnish

In a soup pot over medium heat, warm the olive oil. Add the onion and chorizo; sauté until the onion is soft, about 5 minutes. Add the garlic and continue to cook for a minute or two. Stir in the stock, tomato, and beans; simmer until heated through, about 10 minutes. Add salt and pepper to taste.

While the soup is simmering, warm the vegetable oil in a skillet over medium heat. Fry the tortilla strips until crisp, about 2 minutes. Remove and set aside on a paper-towel–lined plate.

Serve the soup in bowls, topped with tortilla strips and fresh herbs.

Serves 2 to 4

OAXACAN-STYLE RIO ZAPE BEAN SOUP WITH SHRIMP AND CHILE

This creamy, somewhat elegant bean soup, inspired by a recipe from Patricia Quintana, serves a crowd. You can cook more shrimp, if you like. If you are not a fan of shrimp, you can top with fried tortilla strips, crumbled cheese, and/or avocado. We used our Rio Zape beans but black beans would also be delicious.

FOR THE BEANS:

1 small white onion, chopped

2 tablespoons olive oil

1 pound uncooked Rancho Gordo Rio Zape or Midnight Black beans, picked over and rinsed

1 garlic head, halved crosswise

1 teaspoon cumin seeds

3 teaspoons salt, or to taste

FOR THE SOUP BASE:

4 plum tomatoes

1 medium onion, quartered

2 chipotle chiles in adobo

4 garlic cloves, peeled, plus 6 garlic cloves, peeled and minced (divided use)

1 teaspoon cumin seeds

8 avocado leaves, lightly roasted and crumbled (about ¼ cup crumbled) (optional)

¼ cup olive oil, lard, or sunflower oil

2 to 4 cups chicken or vegetable broth

½ cup half-and-half

Salt and freshly ground black pepper

FOR GARNISH:

6 tablespoons olive oil

2 ounces (4 tablespoons) butter

1 onion, finely chopped

6 garlic cloves, peeled and finely chopped

4 to 6 serrano chiles, seeded and finely chopped

16 U10 shrimp, peeled, deveined, and without heads (see note)

1 cup white wine

Salt and freshly ground black pepper

To prepare the beans: In a large pot over medium heat, sauté the onion in the olive oil. Add beans, garlic, cumin, and enough water to cover by about 2 inches. Bring to a rolling boil for 10 to 15 minutes. Reduce heat to a gentle simmer, using a lid to help regulate the heat, and gently cook until beans are tender, 1 to 3 hours, adding salt when the beans start to soften. Remove and discard the garlic head, then puree the beans with an immersion blender in the pan until smooth (or transfer half the beans to a food processor or blender, and process in batches before returning to the pan).

To prepare the soup base: On a griddle, comal, or skillet over medium-high heat, roast the tomatoes and onion quarters until charred and softened, 5 to 10 minutes. In a blender, combine the roasted tomatoes and onion with the chipotle chiles, whole garlic cloves, cumin, and avocado leaves, if using. Blend until smooth.

In a large soup pot over medium-low heat, warm the oil; add the minced garlic and sauté until lightly golden. Add the blended tomatoes and the beans and their broth; reduce heat to medium and simmer until slightly reduced and thickened, about 20 minutes, adding chicken or vegetable broth as needed for desired consistency. Stir in the half-and-half; reduce heat to medium-low and cook for 10 to 15 minutes. Taste and add salt and pepper.

To prepare the garnish: In a skillet over medium heat, melt the oil and butter. Add the onion and garlic; cook until softened, 3 to 5 minutes. Add the serrano chiles and shrimp; sauté until the shrimp turn pink, 2 to 3 minutes. Remove the shrimp to a plate. Add the white wine and cook, stirring, until the wine reduces by about half. Season with salt and pepper, and set aside.

Serve the warm soup in bowls, garnishing each bowl with 2 or more shrimp, and drizzling with the reserved chile-onion mixture.

NOTE: Shrimp classed as U10 (under 10 pieces per pound) are also sold as Colossal or Jumbo shrimp; use the largest you can find.

Serves 8

SUMMER VEGETABLE AND SCARLET RUNNER SOUP WITH GARLIC CROUTONS

You don't have to reserve soups for the colder months. Think of all the summer vegetables just waiting to be put to use in a soup! Serve this al fresco with a green salad and cold wine.

½ pound uncooked Rancho Gordo Scarlet Runner beans, or other bean of choice

3 garlic cloves — 1 crushed and 2 minced (divided use)

Bouquet garni: a few parsley and thyme sprigs, Parmesan rind, and a bay leaf, wrapped in cheesecloth and tied with twine

1 teaspoon salt, plus more to taste

2 tablespoons extra-virgin olive oil

2 large leeks, white and light-green parts only, halved and sliced

2 celery stalks, chopped

1 cup peeled, seeded, and chopped tomatoes (about ¾ pound)

Freshly ground black pepper

1 good-size pattypan squash or other summer squash, quartered and sliced (about 2 cups)

Fresh corn kernels from 3 ears of corn

3 cups vegetable stock

Homemade Garlic Croutons (page 98), for garnish

Slivered fresh basil and grated Parmesan cheese, for garnish

In a heavy soup pot or Dutch oven over high heat, combine the beans, crushed garlic, and enough water to cover by 2 inches. Bring to a rolling boil and cook for 10 minutes. Reduce heat to medium-low, add bouquet garni, and simmer, partially covered, until beans are soft, 1 to 2 hours, adding salt when beans begin to soften.

Meanwhile, in a medium skillet, warm the olive oil over medium heat; add leeks and celery. Sauté until vegetables begin to soften, about 5 minutes. Add the minced garlic; sauté until fragrant, 30 seconds to a minute, then add tomatoes. Season to taste with salt and pepper. Cook, stirring often, until tomatoes soften slightly, about 10 minutes.

Stir leek-tomato mixture into the beans, along with summer squash, corn, and vegetable stock. Bring back to a simmer and cook until the vegetables are just turning soft, about 15 minutes. Taste and adjust seasonings.

Remove bouquet garni, and ladle soup into bowls. Top each serving with croutons and a generous sprinkling of slivered basil leaves and Parmesan.

Serves 4

POSOLE WITH EYE OF THE GOAT BEANS

Beans and corn work so well as neighbors in the soil that a reunion on your stove seems only fitting. You can buy canned hominy, but the payoff from making posole from scratch is well worth the extra effort. This dish comes together quickly if you have leftover cooked chicken and you soak the posole the day before you plan on making it.

1 medium white onion, halved (divided use)

Salt

2 dried New Mexico chiles, seeded and stemmed

2 tablespoons mild extra-virgin olive oil or sunflower oil

2 garlic cloves, finely chopped

1½ teaspoons dried Mexican oregano

4 cups chicken or vegetable broth

4 whole fresh or canned plum tomatoes, chopped and drained

3 to 4 cups cooked Rancho Gordo White Corn Posole/Prepared Hominy, plus 1 cup of cooking liquid (page 98)

2 cups drained, cooked Rancho Gordo Eye of the Goat beans, or any mild, pinto-like bean

1½ cups shredded cooked chicken (optional)

Salt and freshly ground pepper

Corn tortillas, warmed, for serving

1 avocado, pitted, peeled, and diced, for serving

1 lime, quartered, for serving

½ cup cilantro leaves, for serving

In a small, heavy skillet over medium-high heat, toast the chiles until they begin to emit a spicy fragrance, about 15 seconds per side. Watch them carefully to avoid burning them. Place the chiles in a small bowl and cover with boiling water; soak for 20 to 30 minutes.

In a blender, process the chiles with enough of their soaking water to make a puree about the consistency of buttermilk.

Cut one onion half into thin slices. In a soup pot over medium heat, warm the oil. Add the sliced onion and garlic; sauté until soft and fragrant, 3 to 4 minutes. Add the oregano, broth, chili puree, tomatoes, posole, and cooking liquid. Bring the mixture to a boil. Add the beans and simmer for 20 minutes to allow the flavors to blend. Add the chicken, if using, and stir to warm through. Season with salt and pepper.

Finely dice the remaining onion half. Ladle the soup into warmed deep bowls. Pass the onion, tortillas, avocado, lime, and cilantro at the table.

Serves 4

CHRISTMAS LIMA BEAN AND CABBAGE SOUP

CHRISTMAS LIMA BEAN AND CABBAGE SOUP

Cabbage and beans may not be the most glamourous duo, but they have a lot of chemistry! We gave this hearty soup a flavor boost with a spoonful of miso and a drizzle of chile oil.

3 tablespoons olive oil

2 large shallots, thinly sliced

3 garlic cloves, thinly sliced

3 cups vegetable broth

½ head of green cabbage, roughly chopped (about 6 cups)

2 cups cooked Rancho Gordo Christmas Lima beans or Large White Lima beans, plus 1 cup bean broth

1 tablespoon white miso (we like Shared Culture's Butter Bean White Miso)

Salt and pepper to taste

Fresh lemon juice, to taste

Chile oil or chile flakes, for garnish

Chopped parsley, for garnish

Homemade Croutons (page 98), for garnish

In a soup pot over medium heat, warm the olive oil. Add the shallots and a sprinkle of salt and cook, stirring occasionally, until they are completely soft and caramelized, 10 to 15 minutes. Add the garlic and continue to cook for a minute or two. Stir in the vegetable broth and cabbage; cover and cook until the cabbage is tender but not mushy, about 15 minutes.

Stir in the beans and their broth along with the miso. Simmer, uncovered, until the beans are warmed through, about 10 minutes. Taste and adjust the seasonings with salt, pepper, and lemon juice.

Serve the soup garnished with chile oil or chile flakes, fresh parsley, and croutons.

Serves 4

CARIBBEAN BLACK BEAN SOUP WITH ROASTED GARLIC AND TOMATOES

A great, substantial bean soup like this one makes you realize how easy it is to enjoy meat-free meals. A version of this recipe first appeared in *Heirloom Beans* by Steve Sando and Vanessa Barrington (Chronicle Books, 2008).

6 garlic cloves, unpeeled

2 tablespoons extra-virgin olive oil, plus more for drizzling

4 whole plum tomatoes, fresh or canned with juice

Salt

½ of a medium yellow or white onion, chopped

1 jalapeño chile, chopped

1 medium carrot, peeled and chopped

3 cups cooked Rancho Gordo Midnight Black beans, or other black beans, with their broth

1½ teaspoons cumin seeds, toasted and ground

1 teaspoon dried oregano

½ teaspoon cayenne pepper

2 cups chicken or vegetable broth

Freshly ground black pepper

Sour cream, for garnish

1 avocado, pitted, peeled, and sliced, for garnish

Cilantro leaves, for garnish

Preheat the oven to 400°F. Place the garlic cloves on a sheet of aluminum foil, drizzle with a little olive oil, and wrap in the foil. Put the tomatoes in a baking dish. If using fresh tomatoes, cut them in half and put them cut side down in the dish. Season with salt, and drizzle with a little olive oil. Roast the tomatoes and garlic until soft, about 20 minutes. Remove and set aside.

Meanwhile, in a large soup pot over medium heat, warm the 2 tablespoons olive oil. Add the onion, chile, and carrot; sauté until fragrant and beginning to caramelize, about 10 minutes. Add the beans and their broth, along with the cumin, oregano, cayenne, and chicken or vegetable broth.

Peel the roasted garlic cloves, then chop the garlic and tomatoes coarsely; add to the beans. Add pepper and more salt, to taste. Bring to a simmer over low heat; cook until the vegetables are soft and flavors blended, about 15 minutes.

Puree the soup with an immersion blender in the pan until smooth (or transfer half to a food processor or blender, and process in batches before returning to the pan). Taste and adjust seasonings as needed. Ladle the soup into warmed bowls and garnish with sour cream, avocado slices, and cilantro.

Serves 4

SOPA DE FRIJOL CON LONGANIZA (BEAN SOUP WITH LONGANIZA)

This recipe is simple but with our beans and good longaniza, you'll have a feast. The differences between longaniza and Mexican chorizo are up for debate; both are a soft, spicy pork sausage. A simple pork sausage would be an adequate substitute, but avoid Spanish chorizo, which is cured and hard. Also, it would be best to avoid Italian sausages with a distinct fennel seed flavor. This recipe is inspired by the Frijoles section of the book *Platillos Populares Mexicanos,* by Josefina Velasquez de Leon (CEIMSA, 1960).

2 plum tomatoes

½ of a medium onion, roughly chopped

5 tablespoons extra-virgin olive oil (divided use)

3 corn tortillas, cut into strips

Salt

1 pound good-quality Mexican longaniza (see note), casing removed

2 cups cooked Rancho Gordo Moro beans, or other dark heirloom beans

6 cups bean broth (or a combination of bean broth and chicken or vegetable stock)

Crumbled Mexican cotija cheese, for serving

Heat a skillet or comal over medium-high heat. Place the tomatoes on the skillet and cook, turning occasionally with tongs, until charred on all sides, 10 to 15 minutes. Remove the tomatoes from the pan and transfer to a blender or food processor, along with the onion; puree until smooth.

Heat a heavy-bottomed soup pot or Dutch oven over medium-high heat. Add 2 tablespoons of the oil and heat until shimmering. Add the tortilla strips and fry, stirring, until crisp, 1 to 2 minutes. Remove to a paper-towel–lined plate and sprinkle with salt.

In the same pot, warm the remaining oil over medium heat. Add the longaniza; sauté until cooked through, 10 to 15 minutes. Remove the longaniza using a slotted spoon; set aside, leaving the rendered fat in the pan. Add the tomato-onion puree to pan with the longaniza fat. Cook until the mixture thickens, about 8 minutes.

In a blender or food processor, combine the beans and broth; puree until smooth, then add to the pot with the tomato mixture. Bring to a simmer over medium-low heat; cook until it reaches a creamy consistency, about 10 minutes. Taste and add salt if needed. Remove the pot from the heat, and stir in the longaniza and tortilla strips. Serve the soup in bowls, topped with cotija cheese.

Serves 4 to 6

CHIAPAS BLACK BEAN SOUP WITH MASA DUMPLINGS

Diana and Celene in our retail department agreed to translate and test this recipe from *Culinaria Afrodescendiente de Tamiahua* by Dora Elena Careaga Gutiérrez (Secretaría de Cultura, 2018). We all went nuts for it when they made it in our test kitchen! They tried making the orejitas (ear-shaped corn dumplings) with lard and olive oil; both versions were delicious in their own way.

1½ cups masa harina (divided use)

2 cups water (divided use), plus more for poaching the dumplings

2 tablespoons lard or olive oil (divided use)

Salt

¼ of an onion, sliced

2 garlic cloves, cut into halves or thirds

3 sprigs fresh epazote

3 cups cooked Rancho Gordo Chiapas Black beans or other black beans, plus 4 cups of their broth

---

In a mixing bowl, combine 1 cup of masa, ½ cup of water, 1 tablespoon of lard or oil, and ⅛ teaspoon of salt. Knead into a ball and ensure the ingredients are well-mixed. The masa will be ready when there is no visible flour and it holds together without falling apart. This will be used to make the orejitas.

To make the orejitas, form small balls about the size of ping-pong balls from the prepared masa, then make a dent in the center with your thumb.

In a medium saucepan, boil 2½ cups of water. Reduce heat to medium and add the orejitas; simmer for 10 minutes. Remove pan from heat and set aside.

In a blender, combine the remaining ½ cup of masa with 1½ cups of water; blend until fully combined. Set aside.

In a soup pot over medium-low heat, warm the remaining 1 tablespoon of lard or oil. Add the sliced onion and garlic; sauté until golden brown. Add the epazote, beans, and bean broth. Pass the masa-water mixture through a strainer into the pot of beans, removing any lumps; the color of the broth will lighten a bit. Cook for 5 to 10 minutes, stirring frequently, then add the drained orejitas. Return to a simmer, and cook for another 5 to 10 minutes. Taste and adjust seasonings, then serve.

Serves 4

HAITIAN BLACK BEAN SOUP

This soup is inspired by a recipe from the Mika's Table website by Michelle Barbor. It's not over-your-head intense, but you'll find yourself coming back for bowl after bowl.

Haitian Black Bean Soup, known locally as Sos Pwa Nwa, is, according to Barbor, "more than just a meal ... a celebration of Haitian heritage, bringing together unique flavors and ingredients that reflect the island's history and agricultural bounty."

2 cups Rancho Gordo Midnight Black beans, picked over and rinsed, and soaked overnight

8 cups water (or vegetable broth for a richer flavor)

1 tablespoon olive oil

1 large onion, finely chopped

3 garlic cloves, minced

1 bell pepper, any color, diced

½ cup roasted tomatoes

2 teaspoons salt

1 teaspoon ground black pepper

¼ teaspoon ground cloves

½ teaspoon thyme, dried or fresh

1 cup coconut milk

Cooked white rice, for serving (optional)

Minced parsley or avocado slices, for garnish

In a large pot over high heat, combine the beans and enough water or broth to cover the beans by at least 2 inches. Bring to a rolling boil and cook for 10 minutes, then reduce the heat to low and cook the beans gently, partially covered, until very soft, 1 to 2 hours.

Meanwhile, in a skillet over medium-low heat, warm the olive oil. Add the onion, garlic, and bell pepper; lightly sauté until tender, about 10 minutes. Add the roasted tomatoes and the salt; cook for 2 to 3 minutes, then remove from heat and set aside.

Puree the beans with an immersion blender in the pan (or transfer half to a food processor or blender, and process in batches before returning to the pan). You can adjust the texture according to your preference, aiming for either a smooth, creamy soup or a more textured blend. Add the sautéed tomato-vegetable mixture, pepper, cloves, thyme, and coconut milk. Bring the soup back to a simmer, and cook for 15 or so minutes to integrate the flavors fully; taste and adjust seasonings.

Serve the soup warm, ideally over a bed of rice, garnished with parsley or avocado slices.

Serves 4

OTHER LEGUMES

SOPA DE GARBANZO

Steve was going through his collection of Mexican cookbooks and came across a tattered copy of *Recetario de Cocina Mexicana* by Maria Luisa Soto and Murguiondo de Cossio (Vargas Rea Mexico, 1968). Monica in our marketing department translated and adapted this recipe that Soto tells us dates back to the late 1800s. Although the ingredients are simple, they result in a rich and complex dish.

The cloves in this recipe were perfect but they could easily become overpowering, so use them judiciously.

---

5 tablespoons extra-virgin olive oil (divided use), plus more for serving

2 cups chopped tomatoes

½ cup chopped onions

2 teaspoons chopped garlic

Salt and freshly ground black pepper

3 cups cooked Rancho Gordo Garbanzo beans, rinsed (divided use)

2 whole cloves

1½ cups chicken or vegetable broth (divided use)

1 teaspoon Rancho Gordo Pineapple Vinegar

Homemade Croutons (page 98), to garnish

Minced fresh herbs, if desired

In a deep skillet over medium heat, warm 3 tablespoons of olive oil. Add the tomato, onion, and garlic; season with a pinch of salt and pepper. Sauté until tender, 3 to 5 minutes.

In a blender, combine the sauteed vegetables with 2 cups Garbanzo beans, cloves, and ½ cup of broth. Blend until smooth and creamy.

Wipe out the pan and return to medium heat. Warm the remaining 2 tablespoons of oil, then carefully add the pureed Garbanzo mixture. Add another ½ cup of broth and the remaining cup of whole Garbanzos beans; bring to a gentle simmer.

Stir in the pineapple vinegar. If the soup consistency is too thick, add the remaining ½ cup of broth. Taste and adjust seasoning. Ladle into bowls and serve immediately, topped with olive oil, croutons, and herbs, as desired.

Serves 4

POTAJE DE GARBANZOS CON ESPINACAS (GARBANZO AND SPINACH STEW)

This recipe was inspired by a more traditional version in the book *Cocina de Andalucía: Spanish Recipes from the Land of a Thousand Landscapes* by María José Sevilla (Ryland Peters & Small, 2024). We simplified it a bit, mostly so that we could cook the dish in one pot. We also used frozen spinach.

Leftovers are excellent. Consider thinning with chicken broth and poaching an egg in the mixture for a very good high-protein breakfast.

---

1 package (10 ounces) frozen chopped spinach

¼ cup extra-virgin olive oil

1 onion, finely chopped

2 garlic cloves, chopped

1 bay leaf

2 tomatoes, peeled and chopped

1 teaspoon ground cumin

1 teaspoon Rancho Gordo Castillo Spanish Pimentón

Salt and freshly ground black pepper

6 cups cooked Rancho Gordo Garbanzo beans, plus 1 to 2 cups of their broth

1 hard-cooked egg, peeled and roughly chopped

In a small saucepan, cook the spinach in ¼ cup of boiling water until done, about 6 minutes. Drain and set aside to cool.

In a medium stock pot over medium heat, warm the olive oil. Add the onion, garlic, and bay leaf; sauté until translucent, about 8 minutes. Add the tomatoes, reduce heat to medium-low, and continue cooking, stirring occasionally, until the oil starts to bubble. Add the cumin, pimentón, and some salt and pepper; cook for another 2 minutes.

Add the Garbanzo beans and their broth; gently cook for another 30 minutes.

Squeeze all the excess water from the cool spinach and add to the Garbanzo beans. Stir to combine and simmer until warmed through, about 5 minutes. Taste and adjust seasonings, adding salt if needed.

Serve with chopped egg scattered over the top.

Serves 4 to 6

ZUPPA DI PASTA E CECI (PASTA AND GARBANZO BEAN SOUP)

Italians love combining pasta and beans — pasta e fagioli. Here is a version featuring Garbanzo beans (*ceci* in Italian). You can adjust the soup to your desired consistency depending on the amount of beans you puree and the amount of liquid you add. Top with a dusting of Parmesan or pecorino cheese to take it to the next level.

3 tablespoons extra-virgin olive oil, plus more for serving

2 large garlic cloves, peeled

Leaves from 1 fresh rosemary sprig, chopped

3 tablespoons tomato paste

Pinch of red pepper flakes (optional)

2½ cups cooked Rancho Gordo Garbanzo beans or Ceci Piccoli, plus 1 to 2 cups of their broth

6 ounces small tubular pasta, such as ditalini or tubetti

Salt and freshly ground black pepper

In a soup pot or Dutch oven over medium-low heat, warm the olive oil. Add the garlic, rosemary, tomato paste, and red pepper (if using); cook, stirring, until the garlic is fragrant but not browned, about 2 minutes. Add the Garbanzo beans and their broth, along with 4 to 5 cups water (to make 6 cups total of liquid); bring to a boil. Reduce heat to medium-low; simmer, uncovered, about 15 minutes.

Puree half of the Garbanzo beans in a food processor or blender; return the puree to the pot. (You can also use an immersion blender in the pot, stopping when you have a rougher consistency.) Add the pasta and continue cooking until the pasta is al dente, 10 to 12 minutes.

Add more liquid if desired. Season to taste with salt and pepper. Serve warm, adding a drizzle of olive oil to each serving.

Serves 4

BLACK EYED PEA STEW

This is the recipe that switched Steve from passive Black Eyed Pea consumer to a true advocate. It's very simple, traditional, and delicious. New Year's Day — or any day — will be a happy one with this going on in the kitchen.

¼ pound (4 or 5 slices) bacon, chopped into rough squares (optional)

2 celery stalks, chopped

2 small carrots, peeled and chopped

2 small-to-medium white onions, chopped

2 to 3 garlic cloves, peeled and smashed

1 pound Rancho Gordo Black Eyed Peas, picked over and rinsed

1 bay leaf

Salt and freshly ground black pepper

2 tablespoons tomato paste

½ cup whole canned tomatoes with some juice, roughly chopped

If using bacon: In a soup pot, gently cook the bacon over medium heat, stirring occasionally, until it's just done, about 10 minutes. With a slotted spoon, remove the bacon pieces to a paper-towel–lined plate.

In the remaining bacon fat (or in a tablespoon of olive oil if you didn't use bacon), sauté the celery, carrot, onion, and garlic until soft, stirring occasionally, about 15 minutes. Add the Black Eyed Peas and enough water to cover the peas by about an inch. Stir, add the bay leaf, and increase heat to high; bring to a rolling boil, partially covered, for 15 minutes. Add 1 tablespoon salt and more hot water, if needed, so that peas stay covered by about an inch. Reduce heat to a gentle simmer; cook until the peas are soft, about 35 minutes.

Add the tomato paste and the tomatoes. Stir and simmer gently until heated through, about 15 minutes. Add pepper to taste and the reserved bacon pieces (if using). Taste and adjust seasoning, and serve warm.

Serves 4 to 6

FRENCH LENTIL SOUP WITH LEEKS AND LEMON

When the days are chilly and citrus season is in full swing, this bright yet earthy lentil stew will be a welcome addition to your table. A hunk of crusty bread is the perfect accompaniment.

¼ cup extra-virgin olive oil, plus more for serving

1 white or yellow onion, chopped

3 medium garlic cloves, minced

3 large leeks, white and light-green parts only, chopped

1 teaspoon kosher salt, or to taste

Freshly ground black pepper

1 tablespoon chopped fresh thyme

3 celery stalks, cut into ½-inch dice

2 medium carrots, cut into ½-inch dice

10 cups vegetable or chicken stock and/or water

1 pound Rancho Gordo French Green Lentils or Black Caviar Lentils, picked over and rinsed

2 tablespoons fresh lemon juice

Freshly grated lemon zest from 1 to 2 lemons

In a large soup pot over medium-low heat, warm the olive oil. Add the onions, garlic, leeks, salt, pepper, and thyme; cook, stirring occasionally, until the vegetables are very tender, about 15 minutes.

Add the celery and carrots; cook until they begin to soften, about 10 minutes. Add the stock and lentils to the pot; increase heat to high, cover, and bring to a boil. Uncover, reduce the heat to medium-low, and simmer, stirring occasionally, until lentils are tender, about 1 hour. Stir in the lemon juice, and season with salt and pepper to taste. Serve hot with a drizzle of olive oil and a sprinkling of lemon zest.

Serves 4 to 6

ARNAB CHAKLADAR'S MASOOR DAL (STEWED SPLIT RED LENTILS)

Split red lentils are tender, flavorful, and easy to love. According to Indian American cooking expert Arnab Chakladar: "Masoor dal is typically used in South Asia in one of two variants: either whole and unpeeled (these look like tiny dusty brown pebbles) or split and peeled (these span the color gamut from orange to red to pink). Despite starting out brighter, split masoor dal will turn yellow when cooked (and will also completely fall apart). While dals are not soups per se, they're often eaten out of a bowl."

1 cup Rancho Gordo Masoor Dal (Split Red Lentils), picked over and rinsed

½ teaspoon turmeric

5 cups water

Salt

TO FINISH:

1 tablespoon ghee or neutral oil

½ teaspoon cumin seeds

¼ cup chopped onion

1 or 2 Thai bird chiles, minced (optional)

½ cup chopped tomato

3 tablespoons minced cilantro

In a saucepan over high heat, combine lentils, turmeric, and water. Bring to a rolling boil, then reduce heat to a gentle simmer, using a lid to help regulate the heat. Cook, stirring occasionally, until lentils are soft, 20 to 30 minutes. Salt to taste.

In a small skillet over medium heat, warm ghee or oil. Add the cumin and sauté until fragrant. Add the chopped onion; cook until browned. Add the tomato and chilies (if using); cook until the tomatoes fall apart, then mix into the cooked dal. Stir in the cilantro, and serve.

Serves 2 to 4

TERI ADOLFO'S TOMATO, RED LENTIL, AND COCONUT SOUP

Friend of the Bean Teri Adolfo has been practicing Traditional Chinese Medicine, body work, and Ayurveda for 30 years. Her joy is using food as medicine, developing recipes and nutrition plans for her clients. She shared this delicious soup with us; she uses an electric pressure cooker and says it takes her 20 minutes start to finish.

1 tablespoon coconut oil or extra-virgin olive oil

1 onion, diced

1 teaspoon minced ginger

1 teaspoon minced garlic

1 teaspoon ground coriander

1 teaspoon turmeric

1 teaspoon each salt and freshly ground black pepper

½ teaspoon cayenne (or more or less, depending on how spicy you want it)

1 carrot, diced

1 celery stalk, diced, or ½ cup diced fennel

½ cup Rancho Gordo Masoor Dal (Split Red Lentils), picked over and rinsed

14-ounce can full-fat coconut milk or coconut cream

14-ounce can diced tomatoes (Teri likes fire roasted with chilies)

1 cup water, coconut milk, or coconut water (or less, depending on desired consistency)

1 tablespoon coconut sugar or honey

For serving: toasted coconut, yogurt or coconut cream, Rancho Gordo Stardust, toasted pumpkin seeds, fresh herbs, olive oil, and/or a squeeze of lime

Using an electric pressure cooker: Set pot to Sauté and add the oil to warm. Add onion, ginger, garlic, coriander, turmeric, salt, pepper, and cayenne; sauté until onions are translucent and spices are fragrant, about 2 minutes. Add carrot, celery or fennel, Masoor Dal, coconut milk or cream, tomatoes, and coconut sugar or honey; cover and pressure cook on High for 10 minutes. Release pressure naturally or leave at least 10 more minutes before manual release. Puree the soup with an immersion blender in the pan until smooth (or transfer half to a food processor or blender, and process in batches before returning to the pan).

On the stovetop: Follow the same steps as above, but simmer on medium heat for at least 20 minutes or until tomatoes and carrots are soft.

To serve: Top each bowl of soup with your desired garnishes.

Serves 2 to 4

SOPA DE LENTEJAS CON NOPALITOS (LENTIL AND CACTUS-PADDLE SOUP)

Nopales are prickly-pear cactus paddles that you can find in most Mexican markets and some supermarkets. You can often buy them precleaned. When the paddle is whole, Mexicans call it a nopal, or nopales for plural. Once cleaned and trimmed, the pieces are called nopalitos.

You can find Sopa de Lentejas con Nopalitos in certain regions of Mexico. Here is the Rancho Gordo version.

---

2 tablespoons olive oil

2 garlic cloves, minced

½ of a white onion, minced

1 bay leaf

5 cups water

1 cup Rancho Gordo Black Caviar Lentils or French-Style Green Lentils, picked over and rinsed

1 to 2 cups cleaned, cubed nopales (cactus paddles)

Salt and freshly ground black pepper

2 hard-cooked eggs, peeled and split in half

Chopped fresh herbs, for garnish (optional)

In a heavy, large saucepan over medium heat, warm the olive oil. Add garlic and half of the onion; cook for 30 seconds. Add water, the bay leaf, and the lentils; bring to a boil. Reduce heat, cover, and simmer until the lentils are tender, stirring occasionally, 25 to 35 minutes. Add more boiling water if needed.

Meanwhile, in a medium saucepan over medium heat, add the nopales and remaining onion and cover with water by 1 inch. Simmer until the nopales are cooked but still al dente, about 10 minutes. Strain and reserve the vegetables, discarding the water.

Add the cooked nopales to the lentils and simmer another 5 minutes or so.

Season with salt and pepper. Divide among bowls and garnish with eggs and herbs.

Serves 2

FATTED CALF'S MOROCCAN-STYLE LENTIL AND CHICKPEA SOUP

This recipe, combining two different types of legumes with ground lamb and spices, comes from Taylor Boetticher and Toponia Miller of Fatted Calf Charcuterie. As Napa neighbors, Fatted Calf's meats and Rancho Gordo's beans have been long-time friends.

2 tablespoon olive oil

½ pound ground lamb (or beef or turkey)

1 garlic clove, minced

1 cinnamon stick

1 teaspoon Rancho Gordo Castillo Spanish Pimentón

½ teaspoon crushed red pepper flakes

½ teaspoon turmeric

½ teaspoon ground cumin

½ teaspoon ground coriander

¼ teaspoon freshly ground black pepper

¼ to ½ teaspoon cayenne

¼ teaspoon lemon zest

2 large celery stalks, finely chopped

1 large onion, peeled, chopped

2 half-inch slices of ginger root

3 tablespoon tomato paste

2 teaspoons kosher salt

1 cup Rancho Gordo French Green Lentils, picked over and rinsed

6 cups water

½ cup chopped cilantro (divided use)

1 cup canned chopped tomatoes (preferably fire-roasted)

1½ cups cooked Rancho Gordo Garbanzo beans

Freshly ground black pepper

Lemon juice

In a large stock pot over medium-high heat, warm the oil. Add meat and cook for 5 minutes, stirring once or twice. Stir in garlic, cinnamon, Pimentón, pepper flakes, turmeric, cumin, coriander, black pepper, cayenne, and lemon zest; cook until fragrant, about a minute. Add celery, onion, and ginger, scraping any browned bits from bottom of pan. Cook until vegetables become glossy and translucent, about 5 minutes.

Stir in tomato paste and salt, then add lentils and half of the cilantro; cook for 1 minute. Add water; bring to a boil, then reduce heat to medium-low and simmer for 20 minutes. Add tomatoes and Garbanzo beans; simmer until lentils are cooked through, about 10 minutes more. Adjust seasoning with salt, black pepper, and lemon juice; remove the cinnamon stick. Ladle soup into bowls and garnish each serving with remaining cilantro.

Serves 4 to 6

ITALIAN LENTIL STEW WITH POTATOES AND SWISS CHARD

Lentils are prized in the Mediterranean, and in Italy, they are commonly eaten on New Year's Day for good luck. Most Italians would agree that the best lentils come from Southern Italy. Small and brown, with a delicate, nutty flavor and firm texture, they are ideal for rustic stews like this.

2 tablespoons olive oil

1 onion, chopped

2 garlic cloves, minced

1 carrot, diced

1 cup Rancho Gordo Puglia Lentils, picked over and rinsed

6 to 7 cups vegetable broth and/or water

1 bay leaf

1 medium potato, peeled and diced

1 bunch Swiss chard, stemmed, rinsed, and coarsely chopped

Salt and freshly ground black pepper

Splash of red wine vinegar

In a medium saucepan over medium-low heat, warm the olive oil. Add the onion and cook, stirring, until softened, about 5 minutes. Add the garlic and carrot; sauté until fragrant, 1 to 2 minutes.

Add the lentils, broth, bay leaf, and potato. Increase heat to high and bring to a boil. Reduce heat to low and simmer until the lentils are tender and cooked through, 30 to 40 minutes. If needed, add more vegetable broth or water to achieve your desired consistency. Stir in the chard and cook for an additional 15 minutes.

Season to taste with salt, pepper, and a splash of vinegar.

Serves 4

ZUPPA DI LENTICCHIE E FUNGHI (LENTIL AND MUSHROOM SOUP)

This recipe from Southern Italy is prepared with a combination of dried porcini and fresh oyster or cremini mushrooms. Its earthy aroma and wonderful rich taste captures the essence of wild mushrooms just collected from the forest.

Reprinted from *Fagioli: The Bean Cuisine of Italy* by Judith Barrett.

---

1 ounce dried porcini mushrooms

2 cups hot water

1 cup Rancho Gordo Puglia Lentils or French-Style Green Lentils, picked over and rinsed

1 celery stalk, finely chopped

1 small red onion finely, chopped

1 plum tomato, seeded, cored, and finely chopped

2 bay leaves

6 cups cold water

Salt

¼ cup extra-virgin olive oil

1 garlic clove, finely chopped

Pinch of red pepper flakes

½ pound fresh oyster or cremini mushrooms, stemmed and quartered

---

Soak the dried porcini in 2 cups hot (not boiling) water for 30 minutes. Drain and reserve the mushrooms and soaking liquid separately. Strain the liquid through several pieces of cheesecloth, and set aside. Finely chop the soaked porcini.

In a heavy 6-quart soup pot or Dutch oven, combine the chopped porcini with the lentils, celery, onion, tomato, and bay leaves. Add the strained porcini liquid and 6 cups cold water; bring to a boil over medium-high heat. Reduce heat to medium-low; simmer until the lentils are tender and the soup thickens, about 45 minutes. Season to taste with salt.

Meanwhile, in a medium skillet over medium heat, warm the olive oil. Add the garlic, pepper flakes, and fresh mushrooms. Gently cook, stirring, until tender and lightly brown; season to taste with salt.

To serve, ladle the soup into bowls and add some of the mushrooms to each serving.

Serves 6

SPLIT PEA SOUP WITH (OR WITHOUT) CRISPY PROSCIUTTO

After cooking so many pounds of beans, it's amazing to watch how quickly peas and lentils cook. Our Green Split Peas are ready in around 30 to 40 minutes, and you can't mess them up — they're meant to be mush!

The salty prosciutto topping is a nice touch, but not a necessity.

1 tablespoon olive oil	1 bay leaf	Salt and freshly ground black pepper
2 celery stalks, chopped	1 cup uncooked Rancho Gordo Green Split Peas, picked over and rinsed	Lemon juice
½ of a medium onion, chopped		Fried prosciutto, ham, or bacon, for garnish (optional)
1 garlic clove, minced	4 cups water	

In a soup pot over medium-low heat, warm the olive oil. Add the celery, onion, garlic, and bay leaf; sauté until soft, about 5 minutes.

Add the peas and water; increase heat to medium-high and simmer for 10 minutes. Reduce heat to a gentle simmer and cook until the peas are completely tender, another 20 to 25 minutes. Toward the end of cooking, add salt and pepper to taste.

Remove the bay leaf and puree the soup with an immersion blender in the pan until smooth (or transfer half to a food processor or blender, and process in batches before returning to the pan). If the soup seems too thick, add some hot water to thin it out. Taste and adjust the seasonings, adding lemon juice to taste.

Serve hot, drizzled with olive oil, and garnished with prosciutto, if desired, and more black pepper.

Serves 2 to 4

BROTHS AND SUPPORTING RECIPES

BEAN BROTH

There are many reasons to make your own beans, and surely bean broth (also known as pot liquor) is one of the best by-products. If you're planning to make a soup and you've cooked beans from scratch, you're almost there!

Heirloom and heritage bean varieties will create a rich, flavorful broth without a lot of extra ingredients. You can use a ham bone or chicken stock if you'd like, but we urge you to try a simple pot of beans in the Rancho Gordo manner (page 18) and see how it goes. A classic mirepoix is a mix of onion, celery, and carrot diced fine and sautéed in some kind of fat, often olive oil. Adding a crushed clove of garlic and a bay leaf doesn't hurt. You can throw in other aromatics, like leeks and green onions, and fresh herbs, like parsley, rosemary, or thyme, depending on what style of soup you are making.

VEGETABLE BROTH

It's fun to start thinking about what you can add to a vegetable broth. Why not onion tops, carrot tops, corn cobs, or garlic skins? All the things that normally get thrown into the compost might be better served as broth ingredients, although some cooks say that cruciferous vegetables like kale and cauliflower bring unwelcome sulfur notes. Start saving everything in a bag in your fridge or freezer, and make this "compost" broth to use throughout the week when you need a flavorful liquid.

1 onion, peeled and roughly chopped	4 to 5 garlic cloves	Bay leaf
	2 cups vegetable scraps	A handful of peppercorns

Combine ingredients in a large stock pot over medium-high heat, and cover with 6 to 8 cups of water. Bring to a boil, then reduce heat to low and simmer for 2 to 3 hours. Cool the broth a bit in the pot, then strain out the solids. MAKES 1 TO 1½ QUARTS

ROASTED VEGETABLE BROTH

If you have plans to make roasted vegetables, why not roast a few more for stock? You can use pretty much any vegetables you have on hand, but make sure to include at least two aromatics (garlic, onion, leeks, shallot, etc.).

1 onion, peeled and quartered	1 fennel bulb, halved and rinsed	Olive oil
2 carrots, chopped	2 large tomatoes	White wine (optional)
1 large leek, halved and rinsed well	1 garlic head, halved crosswise	Salt
		Bay leaf
		Fresh thyme

Preheat the oven to 400°F. In a roasting pan, add the onion, carrots, leek, fennel, tomatoes, and garlic. Toss with olive oil and salt. Roast for about 45 minutes, stirring occasionally. Scrape the roasted vegetables into a large stock pot over medium-high heat, and add 8 cups of water. (If you can, deglaze the roasting pan with white wine to get all the caramelized bits off the bottom.) Add the bay leaf and some fresh thyme to the pot; Bring to a boil, then reduce heat to low and simmer for about an hour. Cool the broth a bit in the pot, then strain out the solids. **MAKES 1½ QUARTS**

CHICKEN BROTH

When in doubt, poach a chicken. With minimal fuss, you get enough cooked chicken for several meals and nearly a gallon of delicious chicken broth.

A 3- to 4-pound free-range chicken, cut into pieces and giblets removed, or 3 pounds mixed chicken parts (bone-in breasts, wings, drumsticks)

½ of a yellow onion, sliced

5 garlic cloves, crushed

1 bay leaf

1 teaspoon salt

6 to 10 peppercorns

2 to 4 cilantro, parsley, or thyme sprigs

In a large stockpot, combine the chicken, onion, garlic, bay leaf, salt, peppercorns, and herbs. Add cold water to cover. Bring to a boil over medium-high heat, then immediately reduce the heat to the gentlest simmer. Simmer until the chicken is cooked through, at least 1 hour. (Remove chicken breasts after about an hour to prevent them from drying out.) Skim foam off the surface as needed.

Remove the chicken from the broth and cool for 20 minutes before refrigerating or shredding. Strain the broth through a fine-mesh strainer or cheesecloth into a large bowl; cool for 20 minutes. Refrigerate for several hours or overnight to let the fat settle on top. Skim the fat and transfer the broth to containers for storage. The broth can be refrigerated for up to 3 days and frozen for up to 3 months. MAKES 3 TO 4 QUARTS

CAJUN SEASONING

2 teaspoons paprika

1 teaspoon kosher salt

1 teaspoon garlic powder

1 teaspoon onion powder

1 teaspoon dried oregano

1 teaspoon dried thyme

1 teaspoon black pepper

½ teaspoon cayenne pepper

In a small jar, combine all ingredients and mix well. **MAKES ABOUT 6 TABLESPOONS**

COOKING WHITE CORN POSOLE/ PREPARED HOMINY

Sort and rinse hominy. Soak for 8 hours in cold water, then drain. Add to a large pot with 1 roughly chopped onion and cover with 2 inches of fresh water. Bring to a hard boil over high heat for 5 minutes, then reduce to a gentle simmer. Cook hominy uncovered until chewy and tender but not chalky, approximately 2 hours. Hominy usually flowers, like popcorn, when finished. Reserve 2 cups of cooking liquid for later use, if desired, then drain.
1 POUND (2 CUPS) DRIED HOMINY YIELDS ABOUT 7 CUPS COOKED

HOMEMADE CROUTONS

3 or 4 thick slices of rustic bread, cubed or torn into bite-size pieces

2 tablespoons extra-virgin olive oil

Salt

1 garlic clove, minced (optional)

Preheat the oven to 400°F.

In a bowl, toss the bread cubes with the oil, a generous amount of salt, and garlic (if using). Spread the bread on a rimmed baking sheet and bake, shaking the pan every so often, until croutons are golden, about 10 minutes.

PESTO

2 garlic cloves

About 2 cups loosely packed fresh basil leaves

½ teaspoon salt

⅓ cup extra-virgin olive oil

Freshly ground pepper

Pulse the garlic, basil, and salt in a food processor until chopped. With the motor running, slowly drizzle in the olive oil, and process until blended. Season to taste with pepper. Set aside.

LEEK RELISH

1 large leek

¼ cup extra-virgin olive oil

Salt

Trim the leek: Slice off the root end, keeping as much of the white as possible, then remove the dark-green end. Discard the root and save the green ends for stock or compost.

Slice the leek lengthwise and then into thin half-moons. Submerge in a bowl of cold water, agitating vigorously. Let the bowl settle, then gently remove the leek pieces, being careful not to disturb the sandy grit in the bowl.

In a large skillet over medium heat, warm the olive oil. Add the chopped leek and a generous sprinkle of salt. Cook until soft, about 10 minutes, stirring occasionally. Reduce heat to medium-low and cook until the leeks are almost falling apart, about 45 minutes, stirring occasionally.

ROASTED POBLANO CHILE RAJAS

If you have just one or two chiles, it's very easy to roast them right beneath the fire of a gas oven's broiler. If you have a lot of chiles, or you're working with an electric range, you can roast them on a comal or a well-heated cast iron skillet. You have to rotate the chiles and turn them as they char, but you don't have to hover as much as you would with an open flame. Once softened and blistered, move them to a large bowl and cover with a plate, or use a big paper grocery bag for larger batches. Let them rest about 15 minutes, covered and undisturbed. Then you can easily remove the skins and seeds.

INDEX